CHARACTERS

First presented at the King's Head Theatre Club, Islington, on 8th February 1971, with the following cast of characters:

Clegg   Brian McDermott

Miranda   Annette Andre

Bowles (unseen)

The play directed by Jeremy Young

The action of the play takes place in the cellar of a lonely country house

ACT I
    Scene 1   A day in October
    Scene 2   Six hours later
    Scene 3   One week later

ACT II
    Scene 1   Ten days later
    Scene 2   Five days later

ACT III
    Scene 1   Two days later
    Scene 2   One hour later
    Scene 3   Three days later

Time – the present

CHARACTERS

First presented at the King's Head Theatre Club, Islington, on 8th February 1971, with the following cast of characters:

Clegg	Brian McDermott
Miranda	Annette Andre
Bowles (unseen)	

The play directed by Jeremy Young

The action of the play takes place in the cellar of a lonely country house.

ACT I
Scene 1   A day in October
Scene 2   Six hours later
Scene 3   One week later

ACT II
Scene 1   Ten days later
Scene 2   Five days later

ACT III
Scene 1   Two days later
Scene 2   One hour later
Scene 3   Three days later

Time — the present.

THE COLLECTOR

by

DAVID PARKER

M 2 F1 (small)

from the novel by

JOHN FOWLES

SAMUEL   FRENCH

LONDON
NEW YORK   TORONTO   SYDNEY   HOLLYWOOD

MADE AND PRINTED IN GREAT BRITAIN BY
LATIMER TREND AND COMPANY LTD PLYMOUTH
MADE IN ENGLAND

ACT I

SCENE 1

The cellar of a lonely country house. A day in October

The house is a large Tudor one, and the cellar was formerly a secret chapel, lit by a shaft of sunlight stabbing through a two-foot eleven-inch metal air vent above a convex oak door. The stone walls are covered with cases of butterflies. A modern kitchen has been built into a recess between two stone pillars in one corner. A plastic folding door covers a second recess used as a dressing-room. The fitted carpet is scattered with lambswool rugs. The black straps hanging from the brass bedhead in the centre contrast with the white frills and orange bed-cover. There is a large bookcase crammed with expensive art books, and a fussy kidney-shaped dressing-table with an assortment of brushes and perfumes in unopened plastic cases beside an ornate wall mirror. Nearby is a revolving armchair with its back to the audience

As the CURTAIN *rises there is the sound of bird noises, and a distant church clock strikes the half-hour. The armchair moves slightly. Clegg sits in silent contemplation. Suddenly he rises, clicking his tongue in annoyance as he notices a small patch of mud on the carpet. Clegg is in his late twenties, very ordinary-looking. He wears a blazer and flannels with fawn shoes. His air of self-deprecation and well-mannered primness make the occasional flashes of obsessive irrationality all the more menacing. He goes to the kitchen recess and returns with a plastic dustpan and brush. On his knees he attacks the offending square of mud. He rises, checks the soles of his shoes, then returns to the kitchen. He moves to the bed and checks the straps attached to the bed. He sits and slowly ties the straps to his ankles. Lying back, he places his wrists through the looped straps at the bedhead, then struggles violently as though trying to free himself. He freezes as he hears approaching footsteps on the gravel drive outside*

The visitor blocks the sunlight as he stops beside the air vent. The sound of an ancient door-pull and bells ring hollowly off. In blind panic Clegg struggles to free himself

Bowles (*off, calling*) Hello. Anyone about?

Doorbells ring. Clegg wrenches at the straps as Bowles stoops to tie his shoelace. Clegg freezes. Eventually Bowles rises

Anyone there?

Clegg frees himself, flits to the door and inches it open

   Clegg exits

The doorbell rings off. There is the sound of the front door opening. Bowles retreats slightly. Both pairs of feet are now visible through the vent

Good morning. Are you the owner of this beautiful place? (*Pause*) Perhaps I ought to introduce myself. Humphrey Bowles of the *Country House Magazine*. (*Pause*) I—would have telephoned but I gather you've had it taken out? Can't say I blame you—beastly things. (*Pause*) I especially wanted to look at the Priest's Chapel . . .

Clegg There's no chapel here.

Bowles Oh! It's mentioned in the Sussex County History—in dozens of books.

Clegg (*as though remembering*) Oh, you mean that old cellar place that's all been blocked up?

Bowles What!

Clegg Been bricked up. Can't get down there now.

Bowles (*angrily*) But, my dear man, this is a scheduled building—you can't do things like that.

Clegg Nothing to do with me. Done before I got here.

Bowles Look—I'm sorry if I called when you were tied up. I'd be quite happy to call again at a more convenient time?

Clegg No.

Bowles Now look here, Mr—this is a scheduled building. If necessary I'll get an order from the Ancient Monuments people. *They'll* back me up.

Clegg Shove off.

Bowles Very well. Don't think you've heard the last of this. (*He goes, calling*) I'll be back—I'll be back!

There is the sound of retreating footsteps. The front door slams

After a pause the cellar door opens and Clegg enters, carrying a flashlight which casts an eerie glow as he stands on a small stepladder to screw a thick square of wood over the vent

CURTAIN

SCENE 2

The same. Six hours later—evening

The cellar is in darkness. A glimmer of light appears under the door. There is the sound of footsteps descending the stairs. Two bolts are withdrawn. The sound of a switch is heard, and the lights go on. Miranda, an attractive girl in her early twenties, lies strapped to the bed. She is gagged. Her dress matches the large photograph of the purple emperor which now covers the vent area. She blinks in the light and tries to look around. Clegg enters, dressed as before, locks the door and goes to the bed

Clegg Don't be alarmed. I'm not going to hurt you.

Miranda glares at him. She is still groggy from the effects of the chloroform This is your room. I furnished it out special. There's everything you'll need. (*He goes to the dressing-room annex and opens it*) Look, all these are yours. I got them at a store in London. What I did was I saw an assistant who was just your size and I gave all the colours you always wear. What I did was I told a story about a girl-friend from up North who'd had all her luggage stolen and I wanted it to be a surprise for her, et cetera. I don't think they believed me in the store but it was a good sale for them. I paid out nearly a hundred and forty pounds that day. And in here there's a little kitchen. But don't get any ideas, because all the crockery and cutlery et cetera are all made of plastic. And we're miles in the country so it's no good screaming because if you do I shall just put the gag straight back on, you understand. But if you do as I say I won't hurt you. All right?

Miranda nods. Hesitatingly, he undoes the gag. Slowly, he releases her. She jumps up, massaging her wrists

Miranda (*quietly and coldly*) Where is this? Who are you? Why have you brought me here?
Clegg I can't tell you.
Miranda I demand to be released at once. This is monstrous. Get out of my way. I'm going to leave. (*She pushes past him and goes to the door. She tries it, even though she realizes it is locked*) The key, please.
Clegg (*sitting on the bed*) You can't go yet. So please don't oblige me to use force again.
Miranda I don't know who you think I am. But if you think I'm some rich man's daughter and you're going to get a huge ransom you've got an awful shock coming.
Clegg (*amused*) I know who you are. It's not—money.

"Money" strikes a chord. She stares at him, remembering the newspaper headline

Miranda And don't I know who you are? "The Man From the Town Hall Annex."
Clegg I don't know what you mean . . .
Miranda Your photo was in the papers. You won a quarter of a million pounds on the football pools.
Clegg I'm only obeying orders.
Miranda Orders? Whose orders?
Clegg I can't tell you.
Miranda (*in a hard voice*) Whose orders?
Clegg Mr Singleton's orders.
Miranda Mr Singleton!
Clegg I'm not meant to tell you.
Miranda (*incredulously*) Mr Singleton!
Clegg He'd kill me if he knew.

Miranda Mr Singleton—the manager of the Barclay's Bank in the High Street?

Clegg He's not what you think.

Miranda (*moving to the chair*) You mean Mr Singleton ordered you to kidnap me?

Clegg Yes.

Miranda But I know his daughter ... Oh, it's mad.

Clegg (*conspiratorially*) Remember that girl in Ponhurst Road?

Miranda What girl in Ponhurst Road?

Clegg The one who disappeared three years ago.

Miranda I was probably away at Art School. Why—what happened to her?

Clegg I don't know. Except he did it ...

Miranda Did what?

Clegg I don't know. I never knew what happened to her, but he did it. (*Pause*) Whatever it was. She's never been heard of since.

Miranda Have you got a cigarette?

Clegg Er—yes. (*He rises and goes towards a box of cigarettes on the bookcase behind her*)

Miranda backs away involuntarily. He looks hurt as he takes the box from the bookcase and hands it to her. She takes one. He lights it. She walks away from him, smoking thoughtfully, taking in the room. She knows he has been lying

Miranda So Mr Singleton is a sex maniac who kidnaps girls, and you help him?

Clegg I have to. I stole some money from the bank, I'd go to prison if they found out. He holds it over me, you see.

Miranda Well, why don't you pay it back out of the money you won on the pools? You'd have a good bit of change left out of a quarter of a million pounds. Or perhaps you just help him for the fun of it?

Clegg There's other things as well. I'm in his power.

Miranda What's he going to do with me?

Clegg I don't know.

Miranda Where is he now?

Clegg He'll be coming soon, I expect.

Miranda Ah yes. This must be his house in Suffolk.

Clegg Yes.

Miranda (*in a hard voice*) He hasn't got a house in Suffolk.

Clegg You don't know. I came to ask what you'd like to eat. I could do you some bacon and eggs if you like.

Miranda I don't want to eat. I feel ill. And this horrid room's damp and airless. Was that chloroform you gave me?

Clegg I didn't know it'd make you ill—honest.

Miranda Mr Singleton should have told you.

Clegg Are you sure you wouldn't like some tea—or coffee?

Miranda Coffee—if you drink some first.

While Clegg is distracted in the kitchen Miranda goes to the door and examines it. She then goes to the dressing-room recess, thinking there may be a door off. She notices the new dresses on hangers. She returns to the dressing-table and studies the butterflies mounted in plastic cases before sitting on the stool and examining the contents of the dressing-table. She opens a drawer and discovers a selection of underwear

All you've told me about Mr Singleton's a story. I don't believe it. He's not that sort of man for one thing. And even if he were he wouldn't have you working for him. He wouldn't have made all these fantastic preparations. You've gone to so much trouble.

Clegg enters with coffee in plastic cups

(*Holding up a flimsy bra*) How much did you say this lot cost? So I'm your prisoner. But you want me to be a "happy" prisoner. So there are two possibilities. You're holding me to ransom or you're in a gang or something.

Clegg I'm not. I told you.

Miranda You know who I am. You know my father's not rich or anything. So it can't be ransom—the only other thing is sex.

Clegg It's not that at all. I shall have all proper respect. I'm not that sort. Do you take sugar?

Miranda (*irritably*) No. Well, if it's not sex, you must be mad—in a nice kind of way, of course.

Clegg Thank you very much. Cream?

Miranda (*nodding impatiently, then in a hard voice*) You admit that story about Mr Singleton isn't true?

Clegg I wanted to break it to you gently.

Miranda Break what? Rape. Murder!

Clegg I never said that.

Miranda Then why am I here?

Clegg (*involuntarily*) I love you . . .

Miranda sits in stunned silence. Clegg stares ahead, unable to meet her eyes. The Lights slowly begin to fade until only his face is visible

I didn't mean to say it. In my dreams it was always we just looked into each other's eyes and then we kissed and nothing was said until after. Bloke I knew called Nobby who worked in the Town Hall Annex, who knew all about women, always said you should never tell a woman you love her, even if you did. He said if you had to say it you say it in a sort of joking way. That way it keeps them after you. He said you have to play it hard to get. Silly thing is I told myself a dozen times I mustn't say I love you—just let it come natural on both sides. . . . I used to see you almost every day, sometimes, because of your house being right opposite the Town Hall Annex. When I had a spare moment from the files and the ledgers I used to look down over the road, over the frosted glass, and sometimes I'd see you. In the evenings I used to mark it down in my Observations Diary—the one I use for my entomological studies.

At first with an X and then, when I found out your name was Miranda, with an M. Once, when I'd been up to the Natural History Museum, we travelled back in the same railway carriage and I had the privilege of watching you for thirty-five minutes. . . . I used to think of you like a butterfly—a pale clouded yellow, for instance. I used to have dreams about meeting you and doing things you admired and living in a nice modern house and you helping me with my collection. Of course I knew it was all just dreams. I knew you'd never be interested in me. I was outside your class. It'd probably have always been the same if it hadn't been for the money. In my opinion most people never do the things they'd like to do because they haven't got the money. . . . When you don't have any money you always think things'll be different after. But right from the start I could see people—though they were respectful on the surface—really despised me for having all that money and not knowing what to do with it. Behind the scenes they still treated me for what I was—a clerk. It was no good throwing money around. As soon as I spoke or did anything I gave the game away. You could see them saying, "Don't try and kid us we know what you are—why don't you get back where you come from." (*With mounting hysteria*) I remember a night we went out to a posh restaurant. It was on the list the pools people gave us. It was good food and I ate it but I didn't hardly taste it because of the way people looked at us and the way the slimy foreign waiters and everybody treated us and the way everything in the room seemed to look down on us because we weren't brought up their way. I read the other day about class going—I could tell them things about that. If you ask me, London's all arranged for people who can act like public schoolboys and you don't get anywhere if you don't have the right manner born and the right la-di-da voice—I mean rich people's London. The West End—of course. (*There is a pause as he recovers his composure*)

The Lights come slowly up. Clegg laughs

Then one day I went into a coffee bar near the Slade School of Art and you were standing right next to me: I was pretending to read a paper. It was full of people, students and artists and such like. They mostly had long hair and that and there were weird faces on the walls—it was supposed to be Africa, I think. And there was such a crush we was almost touching. I felt my face all red. I stared at the words and I couldn't read. I daren't look the smallest look and you said to the girl behind the bar, "Jennie, I'm almost broke, lend us two cigarettes." And she said, "Oh, not again." And she gave you two and you said, "Bless you." And—oh, I dunno—hearing your voice so near—sort of turned you from a dream person into a real one. I thought I'd do anything to be able to know you—to watch you without spying on you. . . . That was the day I gave myself the dream that came true. It began where you were being attacked by a man and I ran up and rescued you. Then somehow I became the man who was attacking you. Only I didn't hurt you. I captured you and took you to a house in the country where I kept you prisoner in a nice kind of way—and gradually you came to know me and like me and then suddenly . . . (*He looks at her as though for the first time. He is close to tears*) Suddenly it stopped being a dream and began to be what was really going to happen. I thought—I can't ever get to know her in the ordinary way, but if she's with me, she'll see my good points—she'll understand. . . .

There is a long pause. Miranda goes to the butterfly cases

Miranda So. You're an ento—ento . . . What do they call people who collect butterflies?

Clegg Entomologist.

Miranda Yes. You're that. And these are your butterflies. . . . Actually they *are* rather beautiful. All the wings stretched out at exactly the same angle. Beautifully arranged. I suppose they must be rather valuable?

Clegg (*rising and moving to her; thrilled*) You can't really think of them in terms of money. I mean these are the best ones in my whole collection. I did the photographs as well. I mean it might take a lifetime to get another collection like this. I caught them all myself, you see. That's the difference. I can look at each one and remember the exact day and the exact location when I caught it. Sometimes it took hundreds of hours of patience. . . .

Miranda What are those ones called?

Clegg Oh, these are my rare Fitillaries—this is the Heath and this is the Glanville. But I'm proudest of these.

Miranda What are they?

Clegg They're my aberrations.

Miranda (*smiling in spite of herself*) The photographs are beautiful, too.

Clegg Perhaps—one day you'd allow me to take some photographs of you—er, portraits.

Miranda Why not. I may as well be up here with the rest of 'em. (*Going to the bookcase*) And these are your books?

Clegg Oh, yeh. There's a lot of books on art as well as butterflies—I bought them for you.

Miranda (*amazed*) But these must have cost you a fortune!

Clegg A hundred and forty-seven pounds. I bought one of every one in the shop.

Miranda (*picking up a paperback at random*) Oh—how horrible! *Secrets of the Gestapo—Illustrated*

Clegg How did that get in there?

Miranda *Torture, Sadism—How the Gestapo broke down their Prisoners.* Charming! I hope it didn't give you any ideas. (*She throws the book down*)

He retrieves it and puts it in his pocket

Since I'm to be your "guest", shouldn't we introduce ourselves. The Clegg part I know. What's your first name?

Clegg Ferdinand.

Miranda *Ferdinand!*

Clegg Well—my real name's Fred. But my uncle used to call me Ferdinand

and I always rather liked it. You know, it's sort of foreign and dis-
tinguished. My uncle used to call me "Lord Ferdinand Clegg—Marquis
of Bugs".

Miranda (*sarcastically*) He sounds as though he had a marvellous sense
of humour.

Clegg (*with sudden manic bitterness*) Oh yeh, he was a scream.

Miranda Well. What shall *I* call you—Ferdie or simply Fred?

Clegg Ferdinand.

Miranda Sure you wouldn't prefer "Ferdinand the Great"?

Clegg (*considering*) No—just Ferdinand.

Miranda Well, look, Ferdinand. I don't know what you see in me, after
all I'm a pretty average bird—or butterfly. I don't know why you're in
love with me. I mean, it's possible I could fall in love with you—given
time. But somewhere else. You know what I mean? I do like gentle,
kind men. But one thing's sure. I couldn't *possibly* fall in love with you
in this cellar. It's so damp. And airless. I just couldn't live in a room like
this. I couldn't fall in love with anyone in here. Not ever.

Clegg I just want to get to know you, that's all. We wouldn't always have
to live in here.

Miranda Ferdinand—you can't go around kidnapping people just to get
to know them. You might start a very dangerous trend.

Clegg But you see I want to get to know you very much indeed and I
wouldn't stand a chance in London. I'm not clever and all that. Not
your class. You wouldn't be seen dead with me in London.

Miranda That's not fair. I'm not a snob. I hate snobs most of all.

Clegg I'm not blaming *you*.

Miranda But I don't prejudge people. I mean I actively hate snobbism.
Some of my best friends in London are what people would call working-
class—in origin.

Clegg Like Peter Catesby?

Miranda (*shocked*) You know him, do you? Well, as a matter of fact I
can't stand Peter Catesby or his flash sports car. As a matter of fact he's
just a middle-class suburban oaf. Look, Ferdinand. You're a nice boy.
I like you, but I'm worried for your sake. Be sensible. Before it's too
late. I promise—I swear that if you let me go now I won't tell anyone.
I'll arrange to meet you as often as you like. I can help you collect
butterflies. We can go to art galleries and I'll take you to some fabulous
little restaurants where the foreign waiters will just adore you—especially
if you tip well. If you let me go now I shall admire you. I'll always think
—he had me at his mercy but he was chivalrous. He behaved like a true
English gentleman.

Clegg I can't.

Miranda You might go to prison for years.

Clegg (*pleased*) Be worth it. Be worth going for life.

Miranda Please, Ferdinand.

Clegg Don't ask me. I can't.

Miranda How long are you going to keep me here?

Clegg (*with a shrug*) Depends . . .

Miranda On what?

Clegg does not reply

On my falling in love with you? Because if it does I shall be here till I die. Go away. Get out. Leave me alone. (*She throws herself on the bed*)

There is a pause. Clegg steals a look at her, not knowing how to cope

Clegg You—er—didn't drink your coffee. (*He goes to the coffee-table*) Coffee?

Miranda does not reply. He decides to make some more coffee and goes into the kitchen. There is the sound of running water. He peeps furtively through the serving-hatch. He returns with a duster, polishes the coffee-table then the butterfly cases, hoping to catch her eye, break the atmosphere. The kettle whistles off. He returns to the kitchen, makes the coffee and returns with it on a tray

(*Brightly*) Coffee's ready. (*He puts the coffee on the table then goes to her*) Look, I don't expect you to understand me. I don't expect you to love me like most people. I just want you to understand me, if you can. And like me a little bit if you can. Look, I'll make a bargain with you. I'll tell you when you can go away.

She looks at him

After all a promise is a promise et cetera—but only on certain conditions and my conditions are that you eat food and drink and talk to me and don't try to escape or anything like that.
Miranda I can't agree to the last.
Clegg What about the first two?
Miranda You haven't said when.
Clegg Er—six weeks.

Miranda turns her back on him

Five weeks, then?
Miranda I'll stay—a week. Not a day longer.
Clegg I can't agree to that.

Miranda turns away. He kneels beside her. She looks up sharply, her eyes blazing

Please, be reasonable. You know what you are to me now. Can't you see I haven't made all these arrangements just so you'd only stay a week or more?
Miranda I hate you. I hate you.
Clegg I give you my word. When the time's up you can go as soon as you like.
Miranda Two weeks.
Clegg You say two. I say five. I'll agree to a month. That'll be—(*he takes out a diary*)—November the fourteenth.

Miranda (*grabbing the diary*) Four weeks is November the eleventh.
Clegg I meant a calendar month. I tell you what, we'll make it twenty-eight days. I'll give you the three odd days.
Miranda Thank you very much. (*She picks up the coffee, pauses, then hands it to him*) You first.

Clegg drinks then passes her the cup. She watches him intently. Finally, as she is about to drink, he keels over dramatically. She looks amazed. Suddenly he sits up, smiling, like a little boy who has fooled his mum

I've got some conditions, too. I can't live all the time down here. I must have some fresh air and some light. I must have a bath when I want one. I must have some drawing materials. I must have a record-player and a portable tape-recorder. I've always wanted one of those. And I need things from the chemist and some joss-sticks to take the damp smell away. I must have some fresh fruit and salads. I must have some form of exercise. . . .
Clegg If I let you outside you'll try to escape.
Miranda (*after a pause*) Do you know what "on parole" means?
Clegg Yes.
Miranda You could let me out on parole. I'd promise not to shout or try to escape.
Clegg I'll think about it.
Miranda No! It's not too much to ask. If this house is really lonely it's no risk.
Clegg It's lonely all right. Look, you can have drawing materials and a gramophone and records, tape-recorder, books, joss-sticks, any special food. You've only got to ask for anything you like . . .
Miranda (*in a hard voice*) Fresh air?
Clegg No. It's too dangerous. . . . Well, perhaps at night. I'll see.
Miranda When?
Clegg I'll have to think. I'd have to tie you up.
Miranda But I'd be on parole.
Clegg No. I'd have to tie you up.
Miranda What about a bath?
Clegg (*looking around the room*) I could fix something up.
Miranda I want a proper bath in a proper bathroom. There must be one upstairs?
Clegg Well . . .
Miranda If I give you my word I won't break it.
Clegg I'm sure!
Miranda I need a bath now. I feel filthy.
Clegg All right. I'll take a risk, but if you break your promise I won't let you out again.
Miranda I never break promises.
Clegg Give me your word of honour.
Miranda I give you my word of honour I won't try to escape from the bathroom or between here and the bathroom, cross my heart and hope to die in a cellar full of rats.

Clegg Or signal?

Miranda Or signal.

Clegg I'll have to tie you up.

Miranda But that's insulting.

Clegg I wouldn't blame you if you broke your word.

Miranda shrugs resignedly and holds out her hands to be tied

Clegg No—the ropes are upstairs in my bedroom.

Clegg exits

There is the sound of bolts being closed. Miranda crosses to the door, listens, tries to look through the keyhole. She looks around for a weapon to stun him with but can see nothing

Miranda He's thought of every darn thing. (*She goes to the bookcase and takes out the heaviest of the art books, called "A History of Fairy Story Illustrations". She weighs it*)

There is a sound of footsteps off. Miranda stands in the recess behind the door holding the book above her head. There is the sound of the bolts being withdrawn

Clegg enters, carrying a black rope. He locks the door

Miranda crouches in the shadows, unseen by Clegg. He goes to the kitchen, then to the dressing-room, looking worried. He looks under the bed

Miranda Lost something, Ferdinand?

Clegg (*laughing*) What's that?

Miranda (*looking at the title*) It's a history of Fairy Story Illustrations. Do you like fairy stories?

Clegg leads her to the bed. She sits

Clegg Quite.

Miranda Well, I'll tell you one then. Are you standing comfortably? Then I'll begin.

He ties her hands behind her back

Once upon a time there was a very ugly monster who captured a Princess and put her in a dungeon in his castle. Every evening he made her sit with him and ordered her to say to him, "You are very handsome, my Lord." And every evening she said, "You are very ugly, you monster." Then the monster looked very hurt and stared at the floor. So one evening the Princess said, "If you do this thing and that thing you might be handsome." But the monster said, "I can't. I can't." Every evening it was the same. He asked her to lie and she wouldn't.

Clegg indicates for her to rise, then kneels to tie her feet, leaving enough slack for her to be able to walk

The Princess began to think he really enjoyed being a monster and very
ugly. Then one day she saw he was crying when she told him for the
fiftieth time he was an ugly monster. So she said, "You can become very
handsome if you do just one thing. Will you do it?" "Yes", he said, at
last. He would try to do it. So she said, "Set me free."

Their eyes meet

So he set her free—and suddenly he wasn't ugly any more. He was a
Prince who'd been bewitched, and he followed the Princess out of the
castle and they both lived happily ever after. Now it's your turn to tell
a fairy story.

Clegg I love you.

Miranda You need a doctor.

Clegg You think I'm mad. I'm not mad. It's just I've got no-one else.
There's never been anyone else I've ever wanted to know.

Miranda That's the worst kind of illness.

Clegg (*taking a gag from his pocket*) I'm sorry. If I lost you now I think
I'd do myself in.

Miranda Poor Ferdinand . . .

As Clegg ties the gag—

                              the CURTAIN *slowly falls*

                              SCENE 3

The same. Seven days later

*The room is in darkness except for the glow from an electric fire. Miranda
is in bed*

Miranda Ooooh—God, please—help me—please . . .

*The Lights go on. There is the sound of the bolts being withdrawn. Miranda
looks very ill, pale and perspiring. She leans over the side of the bed, about
to be sick*

   *Clegg enters. He looks alarmed. He locks the door, then dashes to the
   kitchen, returning with a plastic bowl*

Clegg What is it—what's wrong?

Miranda (*weakly*) How long have I been here?

Clegg About a week. What is it? What's the matter?

Miranda I don't know—all night I—I think it's pneumonia. That first
night—when I had a bath—coming back in the cold. . . . Please—fetch
a doctor . . .

Clegg Well . . .

Miranda I thought I was going to die in the night. Please—get a doctor
—or take me to the hospital . . .

Clegg I'll get you something from the chemist.

Miranda That's no good. If I die it'll be murder. Please get a doctor . . .

Clegg You'll tell them all about me.

Miranda I promise—I'll never tell anyone. Please help me—I can't—breathe . . .

Clegg All right. I'll fetch a doctor. There's a house with a telephone down the lane. I'll run down. . . .

Miranda Take me to the hospital. It's safer for you.

Clegg What's it matter? It's the end. It's good-bye—till the police court.

Clegg runs out, leaving the door open

The Lights go out. There is the sound of retreating footsteps. There is a long pause. Suddenly Miranda sits bolt upright, listening. She wipes talcum powder from her face and takes off her dressing-gown, revealing street clothes underneath. She creeps to the door and exits. Having made sure the coast is clear she returns and hurriedly puts on her shoes. The door swings to. She runs to the door and opens it

Clegg, who has been standing in the dark, switches on his torch. It is angled upwards. He looks horrific

Miranda screams

Clegg (*laughing*) I'm sorry if I frightened you. I knew you was only playing —talcum powder on the face and all that. You did it very well, but you didn't fool me.

Miranda Get out!

Clegg I'm sorry, I didn't want to upset you. I love you.

Miranda Love! Like you love these bloody butterflies. (*She wrenches a plastic case off the wall and smashes it with her foot, grinding the contents into the floor*)

Clegg Please—no, don't—please!

Miranda wrenches another case from the wall and throws it at him. He drops the torch and runs. The bolts are drawn

Miranda Get out. Get out, you bastard—you—pathetic—suburban bastard. I hate you. D'you hear me? I hate you. I despise you. (*She takes down the photograph of the purple emperor, revealing the wood screwed over the vent. She picks up the torch and studies it with growing excitement*)

CURTAIN

ACT II

SCENE 1

The same. Ten days later

The atmosphere in the room is much brighter. Miranda has redecorated her prison. The bed and chair have new covers. Several vases of fresh flowers are about, and her own sun-filled paintings decorate the walls. The room smells of burning joss-sticks

She has built a shaky scaffolding on the dressing-table stool comprising a biscuit tin, several large books and the cushion from the armchair. Perched precariously, she is trying to unscrew the wood over the vent with a penny piece. She pauses often to listen for sounds of Clegg's return. Were the door to open it would cause the whole structure to collapse. Miranda has now spent a lot of time alone, and she talks quite unselfconsciously to the large teddy-bear currently seated on the serving-hatch

Miranda (*exultantly holding up a screw; in a mock clergyman's voice*) And on the tenth day it came to pass that the first screw yielded up itself. Look, Edward! (*She climbs down the scaffolding and goes to the kitchen, picks up a bar of Lifebuoy soap and returns, rubbing it into the threads of the screw. She puts the soap on the armchair then climbs the scaffolding again. Having replaced the screw she begins work on the next one, then freezes as she thinks she hears a sound off. Reassured, she again attacks the screw with the penny*) Oh, please—come on, you bastard. . . . (*The coin slips, and she cuts her finger. She descends, throwing the cushion on the chair, covering the soap, and carries the biscuit tin to the kitchen, where she rinses her finger under the tap*) Look, my finger's bleeding, Edward. Still, it's worth it. I don't care how long it takes to get all the screws out. There must be an opening of some kind. All I've got to do is put soap on all the screws so they slide out easily, then send him off to London with an enormous shopping list—take the cover off, and wait and pray for someone, anyone—the postman, the milkman—someone must come by. (*She places Edward on the bed and reties the ribbon round his neck, singing softly*) "If you go down to the woods today —you're in for a big surprise . . ." Edward! You've given me an idea! (*She runs to the dressing-table and picks up a small plastic bottle with a handle on the side. She takes the ribbon, hooks it through the handle, and twirls it round*) I'll put a message for help in, and next time I have a bath I'll "post" it—down the loo! (*She takes a pencil from the bookcase and sits on the bed next to Edward*) Now, what shall we put? (*She writes*) Kidnapped by madman, F. Clegg, who worked at Town Hall Annex —Prisoner, lonely country house—Frightened, so far safe—Miranda

Grey. There. That should do it. (*She puts the note in the bottle*) Now where shall we put it? (*She hides it behind a detergent packet on a shelf in the kitchen*) He'll be back soon with the champagne he said he'd buy. That's another idea—perhaps we can get him drunk. (*She replaces the photograph of the purple emperor, takes the books from the dressing-table stool and, as she replaces them in the bookcase, hears steps off. In her haste she drops two of the books. The bolts are drawn. She dashes back to the dressing-table stool*)

Clegg enters before Miranda has time to replace the stool beside the dressing-table, and looks at her curiously

She ignores him. He locks the door, pleased with himself. He carries a large plastic shopping bag and two cameras, one with a flash attachment. He places a camera on the coffee-table before going jauntily to the kitchen

Clegg I called in with regard to those records.
Miranda Why don't you just say, "I asked about the records"?
Clegg I know my English isn't correct. I try to make it correct. (*He returns with a large plastic flagon labelled "Sainsbury's Orange Juice"*)
Miranda What's that?
Clegg (*proudly*) Champagne.
Miranda Champagne. In a plastic bottle?
Clegg Yes. I put it in there. (*There is a hissing sound as he unscrews the cap*) Bubbly stuff, isn't it?
Miranda You put champagne in a plastic bottle!
Clegg I can't afford to take risks. (*He pours champagne into plastic cups*)
Miranda Champagne, in a plastic bottle, out of plastic cups. That really sums you up. You got the best, I suppose?
Clegg (*handing her a cup*) Three pounds seventy-five per bottle. (*He clinks cups, then drinks*) Like Epsom salts.

Miranda lets out a scream and collapses on the bed

(*Coughing*) What did you do that for?
Miranda I just felt like a good scream, that's all.

Clegg pushes the cushion aside and sits in the armchair. He jumps up again, picks up the soap and stares at it, puzzled

Clegg That's funny . . .
Miranda (*quickly*) Let's talk, Ferdinand. You're always saying I never talk to you. Let's have an intelligent conversation—just for a change. (*She goes to him and takes the soap, casually*) I burned my finger. (*She returns the soap to the kitchen*) Tell me. What do *you* think about—Vietnam?
Clegg Nothing much.
Miranda You must think something.
Clegg Why?
Miranda Look, I realize you've never lived with people who take things

seriously and discuss things intellectually. Let's try again. What do you
think about Vietnam?

Clegg You said I could take some photographs?

Miranda Take away, Ferdinand.

Clegg (*eagerly unpacking the camera*) If I said anything serious, you
wouldn't take it serious. I mean, we can't do anything. (*He takes out his
handkerchief and cleans the camera lens*)

Miranda You don't care what happens to the world?

Clegg What'd it matter if I did?

Miranda Oh, God!

Clegg We don't have any say in things.

Miranda Look, if enough of us who believe what's happening in Vietnam
is wrong and that America must get out whatever the circumstances,
then the Government would have to do something. Wouldn't it?

Clegg (*taking a photo*) I don't see why.

Miranda How do you think Christianity started? Or anything else? With
a little group of people who didn't give up hope.

Clegg (*focusing*) What'd happen if the Russians come, then?

Miranda Well, if it's a choice between destroying the world or having
them as our conquerors, then the second every time. I'd rather be red
than dead.

Clegg That's pacifism.

Miranda Check and mate! (*She stretches out her hands*)

He takes a photo

Of course it is, you great lump. Do you know I've demonstrated in
Grosvenor Square, been arrested even. . . .

Clegg You're not one of those!

Miranda I've given up hours and hours of my time to collect money for
Oxfam, to address envelopes, distribute leaflets, argue with miserable
people like you who don't believe in anything.

Clegg Why?

*Miranda paces, very much the soap-box orator. Clegg takes photographs, not
listening*

Miranda It's despair at the lack of love in the world. It's despair at the
lack of feeling, of reason in the world. It's despair that anyone can even
contemplate the idea of making enough bombs to blow up the world.
It's despair that so few of us care. It's despair that perfectly normal
young men can be made vicious and evil because they've won a lot of
money and then do what you've done to me.

Clegg (*taking a photo*) I thought we'd get on to that.

Miranda Well, you're part of it. Everything free and decent is being locked
away in filthy little cellars by beastly people who don't care.

Clegg Try having a demonstration in Russia—see what happens then.

Miranda Don't be so wet.

Clegg Demonstrations are just a waste of time. There's nothing we can
do.

Miranda You haven't caught up with yourself. You're rich now. You've got power. You could use it for good.

Clegg Money doesn't make all that difference.

Miranda Nobody can order you about any more.

Clegg You don't understand.

Miranda Oh, yes, I do. I know you're not a yob in "bovver" boots, but deep down you feel like one. You hate being an underdog, you hate not being able to express yourself properly. They go and smash things, you sit and sulk. You say, "I won't help the world. I won't do the smallest thing for humanity. I'll just think of myself and humanity can get stuffed for all I care." What good do you think money is if it's not used? Do you understand what I'm talking about?

Clegg (*staring at her tipsily*) Yes.

Miranda Well?

Clegg Oh—you're right—as always.

Miranda Are you being sarcastic?

Clegg (*thoughtfully*) You know, you remind me of my Auntie Annie. I got a letter from her today. She's always going on about the way people go on these days. Long hair and all that. Do you want some more champagne?

Miranda Yes, if you have some. Look, for the sake of argument, we'll say that however much good you tried to do in society, in fact you'd never do any good. That's ridiculous but never mind. I don't think Oxfam, for instance, has much chance of affecting the government, but we work for it to keep our self-respect, to show we *care*. Say something!

Clegg (*taking photos*) I know there's been atrocities in Vietnam. There always is in wars.

Miranda *Do* something then! (*She kneels beside him*)

He gazes into her eyes

Look. I went on a march to an American air base in Essex. You know? We were stopped outside the gate, of course, and after a time the sergeant on guard came out and spoke to us. And there was an argument and it all got very heated because this sergeant thought they were like knights of old rescuing a damsel in distress. Gradually, as we argued, we got to rather like the sergeant because he felt so strongly and honestly about his views. We all agreed about it afterwards. You see, the only thing that matters is feeling. . . .

He listens intently. She is very close to him

We felt closer to that American than all the grinning idiots who jeered us on the march. You see? It's like—football. I mean, the two sides may hate each other as sides. But if someone came up and said football is stupid and not worth playing or caring about, then they'd feel together. It's *feeling* that matters.

Clegg I thought we were talking about Vietnam—not football!

Miranda Oh, go away. You exhaust me. You're like a sea of cotton wool.

Clegg No. I do like to hear you talk. And I do think about what you say.

Miranda No, you don't. You put what I say in your mind, wrap it up and it disappears for ever.

Clegg (*feeling in his pocket*) If I wanted to send a cheque to—that lot—what's the address?

Miranda To buy my approval?

Clegg What's wrong with that?

Miranda They need money but they need feeling even more and you can't win that by filling in a football coupon.

Clegg (*taking out a letter*) I think my cheque-book must be upstairs.

Miranda Is that the letter from your aunt?

Clegg (*putting it in his pocket*) Yes. Could you oblige by turning your head and looking over there? I want a profile. You ought to go in for beauty comps.

Miranda Thank you.

Clegg I bet you'd look smashing in a whatchermacallit.

Miranda (*coldly*) What kind of a whatchermacallit?

Clegg You know. (*He rises and pours himself more champagne*) It's nice, isn't it?

Miranda The three pounds seventy-five variety invariably is in my experience. A very good year. And from the best side of the hill, but not *too* ostentatious.

Clegg Pardon?

Miranda Never mind.

He takes photos

(*Unkindly*) Tell me about your family.

Clegg Nothing to tell that'd interest you.

Miranda That's not an answer.

Clegg It's like I said.

Miranda *As* I said.

Clegg *As* I said. You know, I used to be told I was good at English. That was before I knew you.

Miranda It doesn't matter.

Clegg Can I go on photographing?

Miranda Fire away, Lord Snowdon. (*With calculated viciousness*) Tell me about your father.

Clegg (*in a hurt voice*) He was a representative. Stationery and fancy goods. I told you before.

Miranda A commercial traveller.

Clegg They call them representatives now.

Miranda (*pretending not to remember*) Oh, yes. He got killed in a car crash. Your mother went off with another man.

Clegg (*smiling*) Yeh. She was no good—like me.

Miranda So your aunt took you over.

Clegg (*photographing*) Yes.

Miranda Like Mrs Joe and Pip.

Clegg Pardon?

Miranda Never mind.

Clegg She's all right. She kept me out of the orphanage.

Miranda And your cousin Mabel. You never say anything about her.

Clegg She's deformed. Spastic. Real sharp.

Miranda She can't walk?

Clegg (*photographing; totally unconcerned*) Only round the house. We had to take her out in a chair.

Miranda Maybe I've seen her.

Clegg You haven't missed much if you haven't.

Miranda Aren't you sorry for her?

Clegg Well, it's like—oh, I can't explain.

Miranda Go on.

Clegg Well—she like makes everything round her deformed too. I mean —well, she doesn't complain outright. It's just the looks she gives. And you have to be dead careful. I mean, suppose I say, not thinking, one evening, "Cor, I nearly missed the bus tonight. I had to run like billy-o." Sure as fate Aunt Annie would say, "You think yourself lucky you *can* run." Mabel wouldn't say anything. She'd just look.

Miranda How vile!

Clegg You had to think very careful about everything you said.

Miranda Care*fu*lly.

Clegg Care*fu*lly.

Miranda Why didn't you run away? Live in digs?

Clegg (*lying on the floor and photographing*) I used to think about it.

Miranda Because they were two women on their own and you were being a gent.

Unnoticed by Miranda, he photographs her legs

Clegg (*laughing*) Being a Charley, more like it . . .

Miranda (*suddenly becoming aware; snapping*) Read me that letter!

Clegg What for?

Miranda I'm interested.

Clegg They're stupid.

Miranda Never mind. Read it. Now!

Clegg takes out the letter and reads

Clegg "Dear Fred"—that's what she calls me 'cos *she* doesn't like Ferdinand—"Very pleased to have yours and as I said in my last it's *your* money. God has been very kind to you and you mustn't fly up in the face of his kindness and I wish you had not taken this step. Your uncle says property's more trouble than it's worth. I notice you *don't* answer my question about the woman to clean, I know what men are and just remember they say cleanliness is next to godliness. I have no right and you have been very generous, Fred, Uncle Steve and the boys and Gertie can't understand why you didn't come here with us. Gert said only this morning you ought to be here your place is with us, but don't think we're not grateful. This has been a great experience and you wouldn't know Mabel . . ."—(*He turns the page, looks puzzled, then turns back* *and re-reads with the correct emphasis*)—"And you wouldn't *know* Mabel! She is brown in the sun here, it is very nice but I don't like the dust everything gets very dirty and they live in a different way to us and I shan't be sorry to get home to Blackstock Road! I hope you didn't mind what I said and aired all the rooms and linen like I said. . . ." It's not very interesting, is it? I mean it just goes on, you know. . . .

Miranda Finish it.

Clegg Then she says I needn't worry about the money—it's lasting well. (*Reading*) "Don't forget what I said about the woman to clean and get a good one as the young ones don't clean proper nowadays. Ever Your Loving, Auntie Annie."

Miranda Do you think that's a nice letter?

Clegg She always writes like that.

Miranda It makes me want to be sick.

Clegg She never had a proper education.

Miranda It's not her English. It's her nasty mean mind.

Clegg (*resuming his photographing*) Well, she took me in . . .

Miranda She certainly did! She took you in and she's gone on taking you in.

She paces the room restlessly while he takes photographs

(*With rising intensity*) Bored, bored, bored, bored, bored, bored. *Do* something. Amuse me!

Clegg What?

Miranda I don't know. Sing. Dance, anything.

Clegg I can't sing or dance.

Miranda Then tell me all the funny stories you know.

Clegg I don't know any funny stories.

Miranda I thought all men knew dirty jokes.

Clegg I wouldn't tell you one of those even if I did!

Miranda Why not?

Clegg Well—they're for men.

Miranda Oh. What do you think women talk about? (*She goes to the drinks and pours him a large one*) I'll bet I know more dirty jokes than you do.

Clegg Yes, I wouldn't be surprised!

Miranda Oh, you're like mercury. You won't be picked up. Here, have a drink and I'll tell you a funny story. It's all about this hairy melon. There are hairy melons, just like ordinary ones, only with hair. Did you know?

Clegg No.

Miranda Fancy. (*She shakes her hair all over her face*) Well, this particular Hairy Melon lived in the heart of the jungle and he was a very friendly Hairy Melon and very popular with everybody in the jungle. One day he was on his way to the water hole to get a drink when he saw a giraffe. "Hello, Mr Giraffe," he said. And the giraffe said, "Hello, Hairy Melon." Then he walked on a bit farther and he saw a python. "Hello, Mr Python." And the python said, "Hello, Hairy Melon." When he finally got to the water hole he saw this enormous elephant. "Hello, Mr Elephant." Nothing! No reply at all. So, thinking the elephant might be a bit deaf, he shouts straight up his trunk, "Hello, Mr Elephant." Still no reply. "What's the matter? Why won't you talk to me?" To which the elephant replies—(*she sings*)—"I'm shy, Hairy Melon, I'm shy."

She pauses. He waits for her to continue. She stares at him

Clegg That's a song. Isn't it?

Miranda (*groaning*) How about this one, then? Two queers. One of them's just bought a big, flash sports car. One queer says to the other, "Isn't it lovely, dear. All that chrome and everything. Does the hood go down?" The other one says, "No. But the chauffeur does."

There is no reaction from Clegg. Miranda takes two saucepan lids from the kitchen and marches round banging them like cymbals

Come on—get on with it! (*She balances an ashtray on her forehead*) And now for your further entertainment—a spot of juggling.

Clegg You ought to know better.

Miranda (*mimicking*) You ought to know better.

Clegg tries to stop her. The ashtray falls, spilling ash on the carpet. He grabs her arm. She freezes

Let go.

Slowly he releases her arm

Get me the dustpan and brush, I'll sweep it up.

Clegg It's all right.

Miranda I *want* to!

Clegg I'll do it. (*He goes to the kitchen and returns with a dustpan and brush*)

Miranda It's your fault.

Clegg (*on his knees*) Of course.

Miranda You're the most perfect specimen of *petit bourgeois* squareness I've ever met.

Clegg (*sweeping*) Am I?

Miranda Yes, you are. You despise the real bourgeois classes for all their snobbishness but all you have to put in its place is a horrid little refusal to have "nasty" thoughts or do "nasty" things. Do you know that every great thing in the history of Art is actually what you would call "nasty" or has been caused by feelings you'd call "nasty"? By passion, by love, by hatred? Do you know that?

Clegg I'm sure you're right—as always.

Miranda Why do you keep on using these stupid words—"nasty", "nice", "proper", "right". Why are you so worried by what's "proper"? You're like a little old maid who thinks sex is dirty and everything except weak cups of tea in a stuffy room is dirty. Why do you take all the life out of life? Why do you kill all the beauty?

Clegg (*blindly brushing the carpet*) You tell me.

Miranda You can change. You've got money. You can learn. And what have you done? You've had a dream. The sort, I suppose, little boys have and masturbate about. And you fall over yourself to be "nice" to me because you won't admit that the whole business of me being here is "nasty", "nasty", "nasty".

Clegg I'm sorry . . .

Miranda (*shouting*) You're so stupid. It's that bloody aunt of yours—she's made an absolute fool of you.

Clegg (*returning the dustpan and brush to the kitchen*) Thank you very much indeed.

Miranda Well, she has!

Clegg Oh, you're right as per usual.

Miranda (*screaming*) Don't say that!

Clegg faces her, close to tears

Clegg (*shouting*) Well, she never bossed me about half as much as you do.

Miranda I don't boss you. I try to teach you.

Clegg Yes, you teach me to think like you and to despise her and soon you'll be leaving me and I'll have no-one. . . .

Miranda Now you're pitying yourself.

Clegg It's the one thing you don't understand. You only got to walk into a room full of people and you can talk with anyone, but when . . .

Miranda Shut up! You're ugly enough without starting to whine!

He crumples on to the bed, trembling, trying to suppress tears. She looks stunned by his sudden breakdown. She pours a large cup of champagne then sits next to him, pressing the glass into his hand. Her hand stays on his

I'm sorry. Come on, drink this. You're trembling.

Clegg (*slowly raising his head*) I suppose you wouldn't believe me if I told you I was suddenly very happy, would you? Just because you think I don't feel things properly. I do have deep feelings, I just can't express them like you can, that's all.

Miranda Just because you can't express your feelings doesn't mean they're not deep.

Clegg I just want you to understand how much I love you—how much I need you—how deep it is. I mean, you know it's an effort—I mean, some people with you—like this . . .

Miranda (*withdrawing her hand*) I want to say something.

Clegg Look, I . . .

Miranda You wanted to kiss me then, didn't you?

Clegg I'm sorry.

Miranda First of all I want to thank you for not doing so, because I don't want you to kiss me. I realize I'm at your mercy . . .

Clegg It won't happen again.

Miranda If it *does* happen again, and worse, I want you to promise me something.

Clegg It won't happen again.

Miranda Not to do it in a mean way. Don't knock me unconscious or drug me or anything. I shan't struggle. I'll let you do what you like. . . .

Clegg It won't happen again. I forgot myself.

Miranda The thing is, if you ever do anything like that I shall never speak to you again. You understand?

Clegg I wouldn't expect anything else.

Miranda Relax, you're so on edge.

Clegg I'm sorry.

Miranda Oh, God. Drink your drink. I know a bloke who kisses me every time he sees me and it doesn't mean anything. He kisses everybody. He's the other side of you. You don't have any contact at all and he has it with everyone. He's probably a virgin too, like you. You're both equally sick. Don't give me that awful look.

Clegg There's not much else I can do. You're always right.

Miranda But I don't want to be always right. Tell me I'm wrong!

Clegg No, you're right. You know you are.

Miranda Oh, Ferdinand, Ferdinand, Ferdinand. A Ferdinand is worth two in the bush.

Clegg laughs

It's not funny. It's terrible that you can't treat me as a friend. Forget my sex. Just relax.

Clegg I'll try. Honest.

Miranda (*automatically*) Honest*ly*. Do you know what you do? You know how the rain takes the colour out of everything? That's what you do to the English language. You blur it every time you—(*she stops, looking at the detergent packet*)—open your mouth. Did you mean what you said about sending a cheque to Oxfam?

Clegg Yes.

Miranda Do it now.

Clegg My cheque-book's upstairs in my overcoat.

Miranda Go and get it. And a writing pad and envelopes.

Clegg finishes his drink and weaves slightly as he goes to the door. He unlocks it

Clegg exits. The bolts are drawn

Miranda takes the note from the plastic bottle behind the detergent packet and sits in the armchair

Clegg returns, locking the door behind him

Clegg (*cheque-book in hand*) How much shall I make it out for?

Miranda Ten thousand pounds—payable to Oxfam. That's O.X.F.A.M. for mother. Just address the envelope Oxfam, Oxford. That'll find them.

Clegg I saw a wall up in London where someone had written "Oxfraud".

Miranda Oxfraud. I suppose that's quite clever of someone. Perhaps it
was the same person that wrote on a wall near my home, on the anni-
versary of U.D.I., "HAPPY BIR'HDAY—RHODESIA". In their hurry they
left the T out. A few days later someone had added, "Illiterate Fascists
—go home". You could go on for ever like that. As a matter of fact
I thought of adding "Erudite Ethnic Groups—go home!"

Clegg (*looking at her uncomprehendingly, with a forced smile*) Yeh! (*He
writes*) Just Oxfam—Oxford?

Miranda Yes. Bless you, Ferdinand. May I see?

*He is about to stick down the envelope. She smiles admiringly. He goes to
her*

Fancy being able to write a cheque for ten thousand pounds just like
that! (*She turns away from him as she looks at the cheque*)

*He goes to the drinks. She puts the note in the envelope and sticks it down.
He turns and looks at her. She rises and goes to him*

You will post it, won't you?

Clegg (*taking the letter*) Of course.

*Miranda goes to her chair, picks up a book and reads. Slowly he goes towards
her, then reads over her shoulder. She flicks over several pages*

You seem nervous. Have I done anything to upset you?

Miranda No. That's what frightens me.

Clegg What d'you mean?

Miranda I'm waiting for you to do something.

Clegg Look, I've promised. And I'll promise again. You get all high and
mighty because I won't accept your word. I don't know why it should
be any different for me.

Miranda I'm sorry.

*He goes to the photo of the purple emperor and stares at it. Miranda looks
alarmed*

Ferdinand, hasn't this gone on long enough?

Clegg No.

Miranda Won't you let me go now?

Clegg No.

Miranda You could gag me and tie me. Drive me back to London. I'd
never tell a soul.

Clegg No.

Miranda There must be something you want to do with me.

Clegg turns and stares at her

Clegg I just want to be with you—all the time.

Miranda In bed?

Clegg (*moving away*) I told you, no.

Miranda But you do want to have me? If I let you make love to me—
seduced you, even. . . .

Clegg I'd rather not talk about it. I don't allow myself to think about things like that.

Miranda You are extraordinary!

Clegg Thank you very much.

Miranda If you let me go I'd want to see you because you interest me so much.

Clegg Like going to the zoo?

Miranda (*facing him*) To try to understand you.

Clegg (*after a pause; smiling*) You'll never do that.

Miranda I'd like to try.

Clegg (*slowly*) All right—I'll think about it.

Miranda You were going to post the letter.

Clegg Oh—yeh. (*He finishes the drink*)

She sits on the bed. He goes to the door, unlocks it, then turns and considers the envelope. Slowly he uses the key to open it, and takes out the note

(*Reading*) "Kidnapped by madman, F. Clegg, who worked at Town Hall Annex, Hamnett Road. Won quarter million on football pools recently. Prisoner. Lonely country house. So far safe, frightened. Miranda Grey." (*There is a pause. He takes a step towards her*) Are you frightened?

She nods

As long as you keep your word—I'll keep mine.

Clegg exits, slamming the door. The bolts are drawn

The Lights go out, as—

the CURTAIN *falls*

SCENE 2

The same. The room is in darkness

Miranda, on the scaffolding, is removing the last screw. She takes off the wooden covering. Sunlight streams through the vent

Miranda Fresh air—sunlight. (*She looks out, listens, then climbs down the scaffolding and lies on the bed in the sunlight*)

Bird noises are heard, and cows in the distance. Eventually, a long way off, a church clock chimes

(*Counting*) One—two—three—four—five—six—seven—eight—nine. Nine o'clock, Edward. He must be half-way to London by now and he's got all that shopping to do at Fortnum's—and the rest of the stuff to get. (*Suddenly alert, she sits up, listening intently, then relaxes*) Who'll come first, Edward? Postman? Newsboy?

A cow moos in the distance

   (*Smiling*) Milkman!

Sound of footsteps are heard approaching on gravel. Miranda leaps up, shouting. She climbs the scaffolding. In her haste she knocks part of it over and has to rebuild it

   Help—help—I'm a prisoner down here—in the cellar. Help—I've been kidnapped by a madman—please help—don't go away. Help!

Clegg's face appears in the opening

Miranda screams and falls from her perch crying, as—

the CURTAIN *falls*

ACT III

SCENE 1

The same. Two days later

As the CURTAIN *rises Miranda and Clegg are laughing hysterically. Empty plastic cups and plates are on the coffee-table, indicating a "party". The photograph of the purple emperor is now back in position. They are playing charades. The record-player is playing flamenco music. Miranda circles Clegg, flapping her arms and laughing*

Clegg An aeroplane?

She shakes her head

    Something like an aeroplane? A helicopter?

She shakes her head, beating her arms up and down, laughing

    Something to do with flying?

She nods vigorously

    Something to do with flying—something to do with . . . That man—in that film. The one that tried to fly like a bird?

She shakes her head and tries a different approach, sitting at the coffee-table and miming pouring tea

    Is it an eagle? Pouring something? Tea?

She nods, then mimes cutting bread

    Spreading—on bread. Bread and—margarine?

She shakes her head, making signs willing him to separate bread from the butter

    Bread on its own—no? Butter? Margarine on its own?

She nods vigorously, then mimes flying again

    Hang on—something to do with flying—something to do with spreading —I know—I've got it! Margarine—and flying—er—Blue Band Margarine. It's a *Bluebird*!

Miranda (*groaning*) Butter—fly. You idiot! (*She turns up the music volume*) Come on let's dance.

Clegg I can't dance.

Miranda (*dancing round him*) Try. *Olé!* What are you going to do when I've gone?

Clegg I don't think about it.

Miranda Will you want to go on seeing me?

Clegg 'Course.

Miranda You're definitely going to come and live in London? We'll meet some really interesting people.

He picks up the tray and takes it to the kitchen

Clegg You'd be ashamed of me with all your friends.

Miranda I've got lots of friends. D'you know why? Because I'm never ashamed of them. (*She starts unscrewing the leg of the coffee-table*) All sorts of people. You aren't the strangest by a long way. There's one who's very immoral but he's a beautiful painter. He's not ashamed. You've got to be the same. Not ashamed. It's easy if you try. (*She hides the table leg under the cushions at the head of the bed*)

Clegg (*in the kitchen*) Everything I've got is yours. I don't expect anything. I don't expect you to do anything you don't want. You could do what you like—study art et cetera. I wouldn't ask anything except to be my wife in name only and live in the same house with me.

She switches off the music

You could even have your own bedroom and lock it every night.

Miranda But that's a horrible idea. We'll never understand each other. We don't have the same sort of heart.

Clegg (*washing the dishes*) I've got a heart, for all that.

Miranda I just think of things as beautiful or not. Can't you understand.

Clegg I suppose you're in love with that Piers Broughton?

Miranda How'd you know about him?

Clegg I read it in the papers. It said you were unofficially engaged.

Miranda (*laughing*) He's the last person in the world I'd marry. I'd rather marry *you.*

Clegg (*hurrying in, wearing an apron*) Then why can't it be?

Miranda (*trying not to laugh*) Because I can't marry a man to whom I don't feel I belong in all ways.

Clegg I belong to you.

Miranda But you don't. Belonging's two things. One who gives and one who accepts what's given. I can't give you anything because I don't love you. . . .

Clegg (*breaking away*) That changes everything then, doesn't it?

Miranda What do you mean?

Clegg You know what I mean.

Miranda All right. I'll marry you. I'll marry you as soon as you like.

Clegg Hah-hah.

Miranda Isn't that what you wanted me to say?

Clegg I suppose you think I don't know you need witnesses and all that? You know, I just don't trust you one little bit. D'you think I don't see through all the soft soap stuff?

Miranda Ferdinand . . .

Clegg Don't you Ferdinand me. . . . (*He turns, knocking over the coffee-table*)

Miranda grabs the table leg and crashes it on to his head, just as he turns. It hits his right temple. He falls to the floor, momentarily stunned, his head bleeding. He grabs at her dress as she tries to hit him again. She screams and pounds at his arm. He lunges at her. They fall on to the bed, wrestling in an ugly heap. She struggles free, banging her head on the bed-head. She lies still

Clegg rises, very groggy, and stumbles towards the upturned table. He picks it up, together with the separate leg, and exits with them

The sound of bolts being drawn is heard, as—

the CURTAIN *falls*

SCENE 2

The same. One hour later

Miranda, wearing a housecoat, comes from the dressing-room with her blood-stained dress, which she puts to soak in a bowl of cold water. She goes to the dressing-table and studies her forehead in the mirror. She opens one of the drawers in the dressing-table and notices the underwear supplied by Clegg, holding up a black bra and stockings. Thoughtfully, she selects the most provocative underwear and returns to the dressing-room

The door swings silently open and Clegg enters cautiously. He listens. Miranda coughs. Clegg creeps slowly towards the dressing-room, peers through a gap in the plastic door, then silently returns to the main door. Carefully he slides the bolts forward then slams them open. He knocks on the door, smiling as he does so

Miranda (*off*) Don't tell me who it is—let me guess.

Clegg locks the door and straightens the rug

Clegg You've come round then?

Miranda (*off*) How's your head?

Clegg I'm lucky not to be dead. (*He sits on the bed*)

Miranda (*coming from the dressing-room*) I apologize. Sincerely. I'm very sorry. I was wrong. Violence begets violence. Serves me right.

Clegg Fine pacifist you are.

Miranda I know, I'm sorry. (*She looks at his forehead solicitously*) Let me see. It's all right, I'm not going to hurt you.

Clegg Ow—ouch . . .

Miranda Did you wash it?

Clegg Ow—yes.

Miranda Not with antiseptic?

Clegg Oh, come on—it's all right. What's the game now?

Miranda I'm very sorry I did what I did and I should like to thank you for not retaliating—you had every right to.

Clegg I accept your apologies. How's *your* head?

Miranda Just bruised. (*She turns his hand, looking at his watch*) How long was I out for?

Clegg I've been gone about an hour.

Miranda Couldn't have been long, then. (*Still holding his hand*) Wha have you been doing?

Clegg Having a bath.

Miranda Mmmm. I thought so. You smell all talcum powdery. (*She coughs, suddenly and violently*)

Clegg rises and breaks away to the kitchen

Clegg Can I get you anything?

Miranda A very large drink.

He pours two drinks. She takes a drawing-block and pencil from the bookcase

Will you pose for me?

Clegg You don't want to draw me.

Miranda I do.

Clegg What for?

Miranda It'll give me something to remember you by.

He hands her a drink then sits on the bed. She draws

Ferdinand . . .

Clegg Yes?

Miranda I want you to help me.

Clegg Carry on.

Miranda I've got a friend—a girl—who's got a man in love with her.

Clegg Oh yes.

Miranda He's so much in love he's kidnapped her.

Clegg What a coincidence.

Miranda Isn't it? Well—she wants to be free again. (*She lies full length on the floor in front of him, still drawing*) This girl doesn't know what to do. What would you advise?

Clegg Patience.

Miranda What must happen before he'll release her?

Clegg Anything might happen.

Miranda All right. Don't let's play games. (*She turns, lying on her back, looking up at him*) Tell me what I must do to be set free? Marriage is no good, you can't trust me.

Clegg Yet.

Miranda If I went to bed with you? Well—would you like to have me?

Clegg I didn't think you were that sort.

Miranda I'm just trying to find your price.

Clegg Like a washing machine?

Miranda Oh, God! Just answer yes or no. Do you want me to go to bed with you?

Clegg Not like we are now.

Miranda What are we like now?

Clegg I thought you were supposed to be the clever one.

Miranda You feel I'm just looking for a way to escape. Whatever I did would be for that?

Clegg Yes.

Miranda If you felt I was doing it for some other reason—just for fun?

Clegg I can buy what you're talking about in London any time I like.

Miranda Then you haven't got me here because you find me sexually attractive?

Clegg I find you very attractive—the most.

Miranda Kiss me, then.

He kisses her forehead

Not like that.

Clegg I don't want to.

Miranda Why not?

Clegg I might—go too far.

Miranda So might I. (*She unfastens her housecoat*)

Clegg You know what I am.

Miranda What are you?

Clegg Not the sort you like.

Miranda Just relax. Don't be nervous. Don't be ashamed. Put the lights out. Let's just have the firelight.

He goes to the door, unlocks it, reaches round it and switches off the light. She stands. He locks the door

What's wrong—Ferdinand?

Clegg Nothing's wrong.

Miranda There's nothing to be frightened of.

Clegg I'm not frightened.

Miranda Come back here, then. Come on.

He goes hesitantly towards her

Clegg It's not right. You're only pretending.

She drops off her housecoat. She wears a black bra, panties, suspender belt and stockings

Miranda Am I?

Clegg You know you are.

Miranda (*gently*) Come here.

She kisses him, taking off his jacket as she does so. She unbuttons his shirt, slips it off his shoulders and pulls him on to the bed. She kisses him, puts his hands round her waist, and begins to unbutton his trousers

Clegg No—please—I can't—I can't . . .

Miranda You can't make love properly?

Clegg Mmmm.

Miranda It doesn't matter. It happens to lots of men. Doesn't it please you when I touch you? You seemed to like it when I kissed you.

Clegg It's when it gets past the kissing. It's not your fault. I'm not like other people. I dream about it but—it can't ever be real.

Miranda Who told you that?

Clegg Doctor. A psychiatrist.

Miranda What sort of dreams did you have about me?

Clegg All sorts.

Miranda Sexy ones?

Clegg I'd be holding you. You'd be asleep. With the wind and the rain outside or something like that.

Miranda Would you like to try that now?

Clegg It wouldn't do any good. I wish you'd never started this.

Miranda Why do you think I did it? Just to escape?

Clegg Not—love.

Miranda You must realize that I've sacrificed all my principles tonight because I want to help you. To show you that sex—sex is just an ordinary activity. People jeer and titter and make it dirty, but it's not. Anything two people do in love isn't dirty. I did something for you out of a *kind* of love. I think you owe me something. (*She pulls her housecoat on*)

Clegg (*dressing*) What?

Miranda At least try to understand.

Clegg Yes.

Miranda Is that all?

Clegg I don't feel like talking.

Miranda You could have told me. You could have stopped me at the very beginning.

Clegg I did. I tried.

Miranda You must understand. It was a *kind* of love. It's fantastic. We're further apart than ever.

Clegg You hated me before. Now I suppose you despise me as well?

Miranda I pity you. I pity you for what you are and for not understanding.

Clegg exits

CURTAIN

SCENE 3

The same. Three days later

The electric fire is on, the bed unmade. Clegg enters, carrying a bag marked "Boots the Chemist". He locks the door. There is a low moan from behind the recess. He smiles scornfully. Then there is the sound of Miranda vomiting painfully. He tips out the contents of the bag and opens a bottle of Disprin, a box of Kleenex and a half bottle of whisky. Miranda staggers into the room and half collapses in front of the fire. Her face is pale, her hair matted. She wears the housecoat, which is stained with vomit. She crawls across the floor towards the fire

Miranda Oh, God—please don't let me die. Daddy—Daddy—please help me.

Clegg (*clapping his hands*) Very good. Quite convincing.

She crawls towards him. He backs away

Miranda Daddy? Please help me, Daddy. I've got pneumonia. I can't—breathe—I'm so scared I'm going to die. These last days and nights—please . . .

Clegg Very good. Look, I've got some Disprin, some vitamin tablets and a bottle of whisky. It's only a bad attack of flu. You'll feel better in the morning. You'd be better off in bed. Come on!

He picks her up and throws her on the bed. She screams with pain

Miranda Oh! Please—God—I've got such pain in my lungs. . . .

Clegg Yeh, yeh. (*He pulls the bedclothes over her, roughly*)

Miranda I can't breathe—please—oh, please—it's so stifling—open the door—please. . . .

Clegg Oh yeh, I've heard that one before! There's plenty of air in here. Come on, take these. (*He gives her several Disprin and forces the whisky bottle to her lips*)

She splutters, spilling the whisky. Enraged, he slams the bottle on to the dressing-table and flops into the armchair

Miranda Please—fetch a doctor—I can't breathe. . . .

Clegg You'll be all right. Those pills will do the trick.

Miranda I'm dying—fetch a doctor. . . . (*She sobs uncontrollably*)

Clegg stares at her

Clegg Will you let me take some photographs if I fetch the doctor? If I put the lights out, like the other night?

Miranda Oh, God . . .

Clegg You did it once. You can do it again. See, I've got to protect myself. Then I can let you go. (*He jerks her up, lifting her bodily from the bed, face to face*) I must have some photos of you what you'd be too ashamed to let anyone else see. And you've got to look as if you enjoy posing. You've got to pose the way I tell you. Then you wouldn't dare tell anyone. Nothing obscene. Just art photos. I'm only asking you to do what you did the other night without asking.

Miranda It's like a—lunatic asylum.

Clegg You did it once. You can do it again. (*He goes to the door, unlocks it, and switches off the lights*) Look, I'm opening the door—putting the lights out—look, I've left the door open so you can get some air.

Miranda Please—please . . .

Music begins quietly, building to a climax. Clegg rips off the bedclothes

Clegg You think you can take me in with this lark, you're mistaken.

Miranda You're not a human being. . . .

Clegg Go on, that's your language.

Miranda You're just a dirty little——

Clegg You're no better than a common street woman.

Miranda —masturbating worm.

Clegg Yeh, go on. (*He rips the housecoat open*)

Miranda Please—stop it—you disgusting, filthy . . .

Clegg (*screaming*) All right, we'll see about this. (*He straps her to the bed*)

Miranda No—please—please—stop it. . . .

Clegg I thought you was above what you done. D'you know that? But you're just like all the rest, aren't you? You'd do any nasty, disgusting thing to get what you want.

Miranda Please—oh, God—please help me. Help—help! You've broken every decent human law—every decent relationship. . . .

Clegg Yeh, yeh—go on—that's it—we'll see . . .

Miranda Stop it! Stop it! You disgusting . . .

He rips open her housecoat

Clegg Hark at the pot calling the kettle black! All right, we'll see about this—you asked for it. . . . (*He stumbles to the kitchen and returns with the camera, flash equipment attached, and begins taking photographs*)

Miranda struggles desperately, arms flailing, creating a stricken butterfly effect in the blinding light. The music builds to a crescendo

Miranda No—please—stop it—please . . .

Clegg Go on—yeh—that's it—go on . . .

The music fades. Clegg sinks to his knees. Silence. He raises his head. Blood trickles from Miranda's mouth. Clegg takes Kleenex tissues from the box and wipes the blood from her mouth—the corpse must not look "nasty"

He picks up the camera, goes to the door and exits without a backward glance

There is the sound of bolts being drawn and footsteps retreating, as—

the CURTAIN *slowly falls*

FURNITURE AND PROPERTY LIST

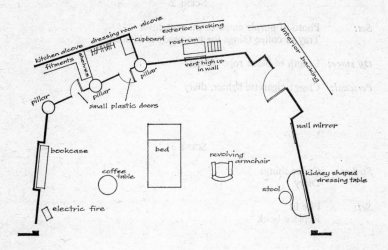

ACT I

Scene 1

On stage: Bed and bedding. Straps fastened to bedhead

Dressing-table. *On it:* assorted brushes and perfumes in cases.
In drawers: feminine underclothes

Dressing-stool

Revolving armchair. *On it:* cushion

Bookcase. *In lower shelves:* expensive art books and paperback
Secrets of the Gestapo. On top: box of cigarettes, pencil, paper,
ashtray

Electric fire

Coffee-table

On door: lock and key, bolts

Fitted carpet

Lambswool rugs

On walls: cases of mounted butterflies

In kitchen alcove: range of modern fittings and utensils, general
crockery and cutlery, all of plastic, plastic bowl, dustpan and
brush, bar of Lifebuoy soap, dusters and cloths, detergent packet
on shelf, tea, coffee, milk, sugar, cream

In dressing-room alcove: girl's dresses on hangers, other clothing on
hangers or in cupboards

Off stage: Torch (**Clegg**)
          Small wooden square with screws (**Clegg**)

Personal: **Clegg:** wristwatch

SCENE 2

Set: Photo of purple emperor on vent cover
          Tray of coffee things for two ready in kitchen

Off stage: Length of black rope (**Clegg**)

Personal: **Clegg:** cigarette lighter, diary

SCENE 3

Strike: Coffee things
          Diary

Set: Fire lit
          Replace book

ACT II

SCENE 1

Strike: Broken butterfly cases

Set: New covers on bed and chair
          Vases of flowers on furniture
          Paintings on wall
          Joss-sticks
          Scaffolding below vent: dressing-table stool, biscuit tin, several books,
               cushion from armchair
          Large teddy-bear on serving hatch
          Bottle with handle on dressing-table
          Cigarette ash in ashtray
          Book near armchair

Off stage: Plastic shopping-bag with plastic flagon containing champagne (**Clegg**)
          2 cameras, 1 with flash attachment (**Clegg**)
          Writing-pad, envelope, cheque-book (**Clegg**)

Personal: **Miranda:** penny piece
          Clegg: handkerchief, letter

SCENE 2

Strike: Champagne and glasses
        Camera

Set: Room tidy
      Scaffolding as before

ACT III

SCENE 1

Strike: Scaffolding, set in proper places

Set: Used plastic cups and plates on tray on coffee-table
      Purple emperor photo over vent
      Record-player on floor by bookcase, with record playing
      Apron in kitchen
      Coffee-table leg replaced by detachable lightweight trick one

SCENE 2

Set: Bowl of cold water in kitchen
      Drawing block and pencil by bookcase
      2 plastic glasses and bottle of brandy or other drink in kitchen

SCENE 3

Set: Bed unmade
      Camera and flash in kitchen

Off stage: "Boots the Chemists" bag with Disprin, Kleenex, vitamin tablets,
        ½ bottle of whisky (**Clegg**)

LIGHTING PLOT

Property fittings required: wall-brackets, lamps as desired
A converted cellar. The same scene throughout

ACT I, Scene 1. Day
To open: Shaft of sunlight streaming through vent
No cues

ACT I, Scene 2. Evening
To open: Room in darkness

Cue 1	**Clegg switches on lights** *Snap on all practicals*	**(Page 2)**
Cue 2	**Clegg: "I didn't mean to say it."** *Lights fade to spot on Clegg*	**(Page 5)**
Cue 3	**Clegg: "The West End—of course."** *Lights fade up slowly to full*	**(Page 6)**

ACT I, Scene 3
To open: Room in darkness except for fire

Cue 4	**Miranda: "—help me—please."** *Snap on practicals*	**(Page 12)**
Cue 5	**Clegg exits** *Return to opening lighting*	**(Page 13)**

ACT II, Scene 1
To open: All practicals on

Cue 6	**Clegg exits** *Black-Out*	**(Page 25)**

ACT II, Scene 2. Daylight
To open: Room in darkness

Cue 7	**Miranda opens vent** *Sunlight streams through vent, hitting bed*	**(Page 25)**

ACT III, Scene 1
To open: All practicals on
No cues

ACT III, Scene 2
To open: All practicals on, fire lit
Cue 8   **Clegg switches off lights**   (Page 31)
          Black-Out except for fire and covering spot

ACT III, Scene 3
To open: All practicals and fire on
Cue 9   **Clegg switches off lights**   (Page 33)
          Black-Out except for fire and covering spot

EFFECTS PLOT

ACT I

Scene 1

Cue 1	As Curtain rises	(Page 1)
	Bird song. Clock strikes half-hour	
Cue 2	As **Clegg** lies on bed	(Page 1)
	Doorbells ring	
Cue 3	**Clegg** opens door	(Page 2)
	Doorbells ring	

Scene 2

Cue 4	**Clegg** dusts butterfly cases	(Page 9)
	Kettle whistles	

Scene 3

No cues

ACT II

Scene 1

No cues

Scene 2

Cue 5	**Miranda** removes vent	(Page 25)
	Bird song, also sound of cows mooing, then church clock striking 9	
Cue 6	**Miranda:** "Newsboy?"	(Page 26)
	Cow moos	

ACT III

SCENE 1

Cue 7	As CURTAIN rises *Flamenco music*	(Page 27)
Cue 8	**Miranda** "You idiot!" *Music volume up*	(Page 27)
Cue 9	**Miranda** stops record *Music off*	(Page 28)

SCENE 2

No cues

SCENE 3

Cue 10	**Miranda:** "Please—please . . ." *Music starts*	(Page 33)
Cue 11	**Miranda** struggles *Music rises to crescendo*	(Page 34)
Cue 12	**Clegg:** "—that's it—go on . . ." *Music fades to silence*	(Page 34)